A LIFEBUILDER

*M*EETING JESUS

13 studies
for individuals or groups

Leighton Ford

With Notes for Leaders

Scripture Union, 207-209 Queensway, Bletchley, MK2 2EB, England, UK
Email: info@scriptureunion.org.uk
Website: www.scriptureunion.org.uk

© 1988, 1999 by Leighton Ford
Reprinted 2003
ISBN: 1 85999 390 7

Scripture Union Australia
Locked Bag 2, Central Coast Business Centre, NSW 2252
www.su.org.au

First published in the United States by InterVarsity Press
First published in the U.K. by Scripture Union.

British Library Cataloguing-in-Publication data
A catalogue record for this book is available from the British Library.

Cover photograph: Dennis Flaherty

Printed in Great Britain by Ebenezer Baylis & Son Limited, The Trinity Press, Worcester and London

Ȣ Scripture Union is an international Christian charity working with churches in more than 130 countries, providing resources to bring the good news about Jesus Christ to children, young people and families and to encourage them to develop spiritually through the Bible and prayer.
As well as our network of volunteers, staff and associates who run holidays, church-based events and school Christian groups, we produce a wide range of publications and support those who use our resources through training programmes.

Contents

Contents

Getting the Most Out of
Meeting Jesus

A few years ago I was asked to speak at the University of Virginia for a weekend on the topic "Jesus Christ versus Christianity." The sponsors had chosen that topic to capture the interest of many students who had reacted against their church upbringing, who assumed they knew very well who Jesus was or either dismissed or ignored him.

It was quite a weekend! Joining me were a very active Black evangelist and a sort of counterculture folk singer. As the students heard the team from different cultural backgrounds talking about the same Jesus, their stereotypes began to crumble.

Before we came, the Christian students handed out a questionnaire which included the request to complete the statement: "When I think of Christianity I think of . . ." One fellow said that he thought of the Inquisition, the Crusades, the Thirty Years' War. Almost anything bad that happened in history he blamed on Christianity.

He came to me at the very end and said, "I was the one who filled out that response. But this weekend I saw Jesus as I'd never seen him before, and I have now become a follower of Christ."

This present study assumes that all of us need to take a fresh look at the real Jesus. Some of us, through familiarity, have given Jesus only a comfortable conventional place in our lives. Others have dismissed him as boring and irrelevant. Still others are fascinated with the person of Jesus and long to know whether he might, in truth, have the answers we are looking for. Like one of Jesus' own contemporaries, they are curious to see who Jesus really is.

This study guide draws on the four books that tell us the story of

Jesus—Matthew, Mark, Luke and John. Three of these, the so-called Synoptic Gospels, are very similar, although each has its own unique perspective. John's Gospel is noticeably different in both style and content. Yet as we read the Gospels, we realize that each writer is talking about the same powerful transforming personality. It is as if four artists were sketching the same person—three from similar perspectives, one from a different viewpoint, with each one highlighting unique details but all vividly portraying the same reality.

Contrary to some sceptics, this study assumes the essential historical accuracy of the accounts in those four books, and that there is reliable, scholarly evidence for this belief.[*]

It is not necessary that you accept the Gospel accounts as "divinely inspired" in order to use this guide. Rather, come to the accounts of Jesus as you would to any sound history, with an open mind and heart to see what you find—more important, what finds you!

The story of Jesus is many-sided. So this study guide selects thirteen key facets of the story of Jesus which disclose his person, his teaching, his actions and his claims. Each study explores who Jesus was and what he can be in our lives today. As the title implies, it is my hope that you will not only study Jesus as a historical figure but meet him as your present friend and Lord.

Suggestions for Individual Study

1. As you begin each study, pray that God will speak to you through his Word.

2. Read the introduction to the study and respond to the "personal reflection" question or exercise. This is designed to help you focus on God and on the theme of the study.

3. Each study deals with a particular passage, so that you can delve into the author's meaning in that context. Read and reread the passage to be studied. If you are studying a book, it will be helpful to read through the entire book prior to the first study. The questions are written using the language of the New International Version, so you may wish to use that version of the Bible. The New Revised Standard Version is also recommended.

4. This is an inductive Bible study, designed to help you discover for yourself what Scripture is saying. The study includes three types of questions. *Observation* questions ask about the basic facts: who, what, when, where and how. *Interpretation* questions delve into the meaning of the passage. *Application* questions help you discover the implications of the text for growing in Christ. These three keys unlock the treasures of Scripture.

Write your answers to the questions in the spaces provided or in a personal journal. Writing can bring clarity and deeper understanding of yourself and of God's Word.

5. It might be good to have a Bible dictionary handy. Use it to look up any unfamiliar words, names or places.

6. Use the prayer suggestion to guide you in thanking God for what you have learned and to pray about the applications that have come to mind.

7. You may want to go on to the suggestion under "Now or Later," or you may want to use that idea for your next study.

Suggestions for Members of a Group Study

1. Come to the study prepared. Follow the suggestions for individual study mentioned above. You will find that careful preparation will greatly enrich your time spent in group discussion.

2. Be willing to participate in the discussion. The leader of your group will not be lecturing. Instead, he or she will be encouraging the members of the group to discuss what they have learned. The leader will be asking the questions that are found in this guide.

3. Stick to the topic being discussed. Your answers should be based on the verses that are the focus of the discussion and not on outside authorities such as commentaries or speakers. These studies focus on a particular passage of Scripture. Only rarely should you refer to other portions of the Bible. This allows for everyone to participate in in-depth study on equal ground.

4. Be sensitive to the other members of the group. Listen attentively when they describe what they have learned. You may be surprised by their insights! Each question assumes a variety of answers. Many questions do not have "right" answers, particularly questions that aim at meaning or application. Instead the questions push us to explore the passage more thoroughly.

When possible, link what you say to the comments of others. Also, be affirming whenever you can. This will encourage some of the more hesitant members of the group to participate.

5. Be careful not to dominate the discussion. We are sometimes so eager to express our thoughts that we leave little opportunity for others to respond. By all means participate! But allow others to do so too.

6. Expect God to teach you through the passage being discussed and through the other members of the group. Pray that you will have an enjoyable and profitable time together, but also that as a result of the study you will find ways that you can take action individually and/or as a group.

7. Remember that anything said in the group is considered confidential and should not be discussed outside the group unless specific permission is given to do so.

8. If you are the group leader, you will find additional suggestions at the back of the guide.

---

*See, for example, F. F. Bruce, *The New Testament Documents: Are They Reliable?* (InterVarsity Press, 1960).

1

The Real Jesus

Mark 1:9-45

We have a daughter named Debbie and a son named Kevin. (Our other son, Sandy, died when he was twenty-one.) Their co-workers and friends could give you some idea of who they are. But I could tell you what they are really like! I know them well.

GROUP DISCUSSION. Write down three facts about yourself on a piece of paper and put them into a hat. Each person then draws out a paper and tries to guess who the writer is.

PERSONAL REFLECTION. When have you had the wrong impression about someone when you first met them?

Most people have some half-formed picture of Jesus—a good man, a great teacher, an embodiment of "the force" or perhaps even a divine figure. Mark, one of the first followers of Jesus, wrote his book to tell us what Jesus was really like. He and Peter, from whom he got his information, knew Jesus well. His opening words tell us abruptly that his story is the gospel—literally, "good news"—about "Jesus Christ, the Son of God." His first chapter tells us how Jesus was identified and introduced to the people of his time. *Read Mark 1:9-45.*

1. What activities does Jesus get involved in throughout this passage?

2. John baptized people who confessed their sins. If Jesus was the Son of God, why do you think he was baptized (vv. 9-11) and then tempted (vv. 12-13)?

---

3. How do you feel about the fact that Jesus was one of us?

---

4. Jesus' first action is to proclaim that "the kingdom of God is near" (vv. 14-15). Why was this good news?

---

5. Some working fishermen, who were not likely to be very religious, are Jesus' first followers (vv. 16-20). Why do you think they follow him with so little persuasion or information?

---

6. How much does a person need to know to start following Jesus?

---

7. Jesus' dynamic authority becomes apparent as he helps people (see vv. 21-34). What words or actions show his authority?

8. What does Mark 1:35 reveal about the source of Jesus' authority?

What can we learn from his example here?

---

9. When everyone was looking for him, Jesus left (vv. 36-39). Why then do you think he stops and touches one man with leprosy (vv. 40-45)?

---

10. Mark clearly wants to tell us who Jesus is. Yet Jesus himself seems strangely reluctant to reveal his identity (vv. 34, 43-44). (Later he's much more open.) Why this hesitance now?

---

11. How would you summarize the way this chapter describes Jesus, and what impresses or puzzles you most? Explain.

Ask God to help you understand who Jesus is.

Now or Later

Read Mark 1:1-8. Jesus' identity is affirmed by three witnesses: Isaiah (vv. 2-3), John the Baptist (vv. 4-8) and a voice from heaven (vv. 10-11). What does each tell us about him?

2

The Surprising Jesus

Luke 5:17-32

Most people assume they know Jesus. Imagine that you go to a busy place near where you live. You survey people, asking them, "Do you know who Jesus Christ was?" Most people would say yes. When you ask them for details, they give you some, maybe suggesting he was a great moral teacher or the founder of Christianity. Some might even say he was the Son of God. But for any of us, reading about Jesus always brings surprises, even when we already know a lot about him.

GROUP DISCUSSION. Think back to when you first learned about Jesus Christ. What did you think he was like?

PERSONAL REFLECTION. How would you like Jesus to surprise you?

The Jesus we meet in Luke's story had a wonderful unpredictability. The people of his day thought God loved good people; he showed a God who loved sinners. They thought God liked sad faces; he showed a God who created joy. They thought God was bound up in tradition;

he showed a God who desired freshness. Luke 5 illustrates what an early Christian missionary told the king of England when he asked what they could expect if they followed this new faith: "Your Majesty," he replied, "you will find surprise after surprise—and every surprise is good!" *Read Luke 5:17-26.*

---

1. Try to imagine the scene. As the paralyzed man is lowered through the roof, how do you think each of the main characters feels (the sick man, his friends, the onlookers, the Pharisees and teachers of the law vv. 17-19)?

---

2. How does Jesus surprise everyone in dealing with the sick man (v. 20)?

---

3. What does this tell us about Jesus and how he sees our needs?

---

4. The teachers criticize Jesus for promising forgiveness, since only God has that authority (v. 21). What is Jesus' response meant to show (vv. 22-26)?

5. *Read Luke 5:27-32.* Why is it surprising that Jesus calls Levi (vv. 27-28)?

Why is it even more surprising that Levi follows?

6. When Levi throws a party for his friends, the religious leaders criticize Jesus for eating with "sinners" (v. 30). How does Jesus' picture of himself as a "doctor" challenge their view of God?

7. What misconceptions about God might keep Jesus from being meaningful to us?

8. Later Levi, also called Matthew, wrote a Gospel in which he called Jesus a "friend of sinners." What tension might exist between being both a "friend" and a "doctor"?

9. What is your overriding impression of Jesus in this chapter?

10. How does it differ from your answer to question 1?

Ask Jesus to surprise you by calling you to himself, even though none of us deserve it. Then ask him to forgive and heal you so you can live the life he wants for you.

Now or Later

11. *Read Luke 5:33-39.* When Jesus is criticized for not making his disciples fast (v. 33), he describes himself as a bridegroom (vv. 34-35). What does this say about his relationship with his followers and how he wants them to be?

12. Again Jesus uses picture language to make his point (vv. 36-39). What do the new cloth and the new wine symbolize?

What do the old garment and old wineskins stand for?

13. What do these illustrations say about how Jesus makes people and things new?

3

Jesus the Storytelling Teacher

Mark 4:1-25

Master teachers learn how to "draw out." *The Foxfire Book of Appalachian Folklore* came from a teacher in the Georgia mountains who gave his students hands-on experience in creating projects. In so doing he drew out their desire to acquire the knowledge and skills they needed. So Jesus in his parables intrigues us to want to know and grow.

GROUP DISCUSSION. Describe the best teacher you've ever known. How did he or she stimulate you to learn?

PERSONAL REFLECTION. When has a teaching method sparked your interest in learning?

Jesus explained things over and over. He did it by using parables that drew out the real seekers and kept away those who were merely curious. A "parable" (literally, something thrown alongside) was a story that both lit up and yet hid truth, depending on the hearer's response. *Read Mark 4:1-25.*

---

1. What do the illustrations Jesus uses have in common with his hearers?

2. What does Jesus' choice of illustrations say about him?

3. Jesus gets into a boat because the crowd is large. Who are the two groups listening to him (vv. 1, 10-12), and what makes them different?

4. Look again at verses 3-8 and 14-20. What is the meaning of the various elements in the parable: seed, soils, birds, sun and thorns?

5. How many times does Jesus talk about "hearing" in this chapter?

How does the repetition of this word help us to understand the real theme of these parables?

6. Are you open to "hearing" Jesus? Explain.

7. It's puzzling that Jesus used parables to prevent outsiders from seeing (vv. 10-12). But as a good teacher, he must have had a reason. What do you think that might have been?

8. What is Jesus saying in the metaphor of the lamp (vv. 21-25)?

---

9. What hides truth, as a bowl conceals light? (Verses 24 and 25 give a hint.)

---

10. Thinking back over the stories in this chapter—the seed and soils, the lamp—which relates most to where you are spiritually, and why?

Ask Jesus to help you understand his parables. Ask him to make you good soil where his seed can grow.

Now or Later

Read Mark 4:26-34. Jesus tells two stories about growth. How would you explain each one in your own words?

Of all you've learned about Jesus in this study, what stands out most clearly?

What puzzles or disturbs you?

4

Jesus the Master over Fear

Luke 8:22-39

Next to love, fear is our most common emotion. Some say our most widespread fears are of snakes and public speaking. Fear of the unknown is even more unnerving. Our Debbie used to take a running jump onto the bed when she was a little girl because she was scared of the dark underneath!

More seriously, many of us are at least semi-crippled by our phobias, anxieties and a whole list of other fears—of ourselves, love, rejection, failure, life, death, the future, even a wrongful fear of God.

GROUP DISCUSSION. Describe an experience you've had of being immobilized by fear. Were you able to overcome it? Why or why not?

PERSONAL REFLECTION. What is a fear you have that you wouldn't want to admit? How do you live with that fear?

As Jesus showed his authority over illness, sin and warped tradition, so now he demonstrates his masterly power over the fears that may keep us from finding life in him or fully following his way. *Read Luke 8:22-39.*

---

1. Luke records two stories here about Jesus and fear. What two situations caused people to fear?

2. In what ways do you connect with the people's fears?

3. In these stories Jesus counters fear with questions (vv. 25, 30). Why do you think Jesus used this method?

4. How is Jesus using a question to counter fear in verse 25?

5. A different challenge comes on the scene in verses 26-39: a man with an evil spirit. In what ways had the evil spirit spoiled this man's life?

6. The demons knew who Jesus was and cried out (v. 28). Why do you think Jesus again meets fear with a question?

7. You would think the people would be glad their neighbor was changed for the better. Instead, they want Jesus to go (v. 37). Why?

Can you think of any similar reactions today? Explain.

8. Jesus doesn't let the man come with him but tells him to "return home and tell how much God has done for you" (vv. 38-39). What could you tell others about what Jesus has done for you?

9. What patterns do you see in the way Jesus deals with fear?

10. Think of an underlying fear that may be keeping you from living the way God wants you to. How do you picture Jesus dealing with that fear?

Pray that Jesus will help you face your fears with his wise questions.

Now or Later

11. *Read Luke 8:40-56.* Imagine Jairus's frustration when Jesus is on his way to help the dying daughter, and a woman stops him. Why does she tremble when Jesus asks who touched him (vv. 45-47)?

12. Jairus shows faith in Jesus (vv. 40-42). How does Jesus use the delay with the woman to challenge and strengthen Jairus's faith (vv. 49-50)?

13. Note how Luke describes Jesus' actions in healing the girl (vv. 51-56). How does Jesus respond in the face of death, our last great fear?

5

Jesus the Challenging Saviour

Mark 8:22-38

Sometimes I think we should stop using the term *Christian*. It carries a great deal of negative cultural baggage. In some societies everyone assumes they are Christians unless they happen to belong to some other religion. In other cultures "Christians" may be viewed as a political party—or even the ones lobbing the bombs! Perhaps it would be better if we simply talked about being followers of Jesus.

GROUP DISCUSSION. We live in an age of unprecedented communication about Jesus. Why then do you think so many people are still unclear about Jesus and what it means to follow him?

PERSONAL REFLECTION. What questions do you have about who Jesus is and what it means to follow him? If those questions were answered, would it change your position regarding Jesus?

Do we see Jesus clearly enough to follow him? This passage begins with Jesus healing a blind man—in two stages! Like this blind man, would-be followers of Jesus may need a "second touch" to see him clearly. *Read Mark 8:22-38.*

---

1. What unusual steps does Jesus take in healing the blind man (vv. 22-26)?

---

2. Why might people have thought Jesus was John the Baptist, Elijah or one of the prophets (vv. 27-28)?

---

3. What half-truths about Jesus are widespread in society today?

---

4. Peter's statement "You are the Christ" (v. 29) has been called the confession that makes a person a true follower of Jesus. Why? (Compare Matthew 16:15-17 and John 6:68-69.)

---

5. Why do you think Peter rebukes Jesus (v. 32)?

---

6. Why do you think Jesus then rebukes Peter so strongly (v. 33)?

7. How does the way Peter sees Jesus (vv. 29-32) compare to the two-stage healing of the blind man (vv. 23-25)?

8. Jesus states that the cross is a "must" for us (vv. 34-38). Practically speaking, what does it mean to deny ourselves, take up our cross and follow him?

9. It has been said that "it costs nothing to become a Christian but everything to be a Christian." How is this supported by Christ's teaching here (vv. 34-38)?

10. "I'd like to follow Christ, but I think it will cost too much." How would you respond to such a statement in the light of verses 34-38?

If you know Jesus but have not understood him well, ask him for a second touch. If you don't know Jesus, ask him for a better understanding of who he is.

Now or Later

In this passage, for the first time Jesus tells his disciples that "the Son of Man . . . must be killed" (v. 31). *Read Isaiah 53.* Why was the cross a "must" for Jesus?

6

Jesus the Source of Power

Life is not always simple. Much as we would like it to come in neat packages, life in the raw is full of paradox. As a result we often find our reason and emotions at odds. It is a mark of reality that the Jesus we meet is both a servant and a powerful leader, both weak and strong. He suffers, but he's also very much in charge. Immediately after the prediction of his rejection and death, the story moves to the promise of a kingdom that will come with power.

GROUP DISCUSSION. When you think of power, who or what do you think of?

PERSONAL REFLECTION. What is the most powerful reality you can imagine? Do you think Jesus is more or less powerful than that? Why?

The paradox of humiliation and exaltation is the precise point at which the drama of Jesus grips us. When we isolate Jesus from the real world, we have only empty words. But when his person touches human problems, power is born. *Read Mark 9:2-32.*

---

1. How does Jesus' power show through his humble exterior in this passage?

2. Imagine you were Peter, James or John. How would you describe what happened on the mountain to someone who wasn't there (vv. 2-8)? (What did you see, hear, feel?)

3. How would it help the disciples—including us today—to see this glimpse of Jesus and the kingdom in power and glory?

4. What words would you use to describe the situation Jesus faced when he came down from the mountain (vv. 14-18)?

5. Jesus expresses his frustration in verse 19, "O unbelieving generation . . . how long shall I stay with you?" Who do you think he is frustrated with? Why?

6. How would Jesus' reply to the father's request (v. 23) both challenge and encourage him?

How does the promise "Everything is possible for him who believes" challenge and encourage you?

7. Immediately the father exclaims: "I do believe; help me overcome my unbelief!" (v. 24). What impresses you about his response?

---

8. In this passage Jesus' followers are confused (vv. 10-11, 18, 28, 32). What is most confusing to you in your journey with Jesus?

---

9. Think back through the progression from the mountain to the scene in the valley. Who do you most identify with—Jesus' followers, the father or the boy? Explain.

---

10. What area of your life has the greatest need for God's power?

Pray to understand God's power better. Pray that God will touch your life and the lives of those around you with that power.

Now or Later

11. After being questioned by Jesus, the boy's father asked, "But if you can do anything, take pity on us and help us" (vv. 20-22). Do you think this was genuine faith? Explain.

---

12. What does this story suggest is the way from unbelief to faith?

7

Jesus & a Rich Man

Luke 18:15-30

A group of affluent Christians call themselves "The Fellowship of Bruised Camels." Their name is borrowed from Jesus' famous saying that it is easier for "a camel to go through the eye of a needle" than for a rich person to enter God's kingdom.

These well-off Christians humorously see themselves as "bruised camels" who want to follow Jesus faithfully but often find their wealth a burden. How much money should they make, keep, spend, give away? Questions like these become very pointed when we meet Jesus.

GROUP DISCUSSION. Do you ever dream about coming into a large amount of money, maybe through a surprise inheritance or winning the lottery? How would you spend the money if you got it like that?

PERSONAL REFLECTION. When you have time to think and be quiet, what keeps entering your mind over and over like a ball on a rubber string? Would you say that was "number one" in your life? Why or why not?

When the rich young man in Luke 18 met Jesus, his wealth was called into question—and much more. His story prompts us to ask ourselves whether we will let anything other than God be number one in our lives. *Read Luke 18:15-30.*

---

1. In this passage Jesus says many things which are hard to understand. Identify each one and tell why it's hard to understand.

---

2. The ruler asks the most important question of all (v. 18). Yet what false assumptions does his question reveal?

---

3. What is Jesus implying about himself when he says no one is good but God (v. 19)?

---

4. "All these I have kept" (v. 21). Do you think the man was telling the truth or was he fooling himself? Explain.

---

5. The five commands mentioned are only part of the Ten Commandments. Which ones did Jesus leave out (see Exodus 20:1-17), and how is that significant?

6. "You still lack one thing. Sell everything you have and give to the poor" (v. 22). So far as we know, this is the only rich man who was told to do that. Why this command to this man?

7. What is hindering you from following Christ?

8. When the man went away sad, Jesus said: "How hard it is for the rich to enter the kingdom of God!" (v. 24). Why is it so hard?

9. According to Jesus, salvation is not only "hard" but "*impossible with men*" (v. 27). Why?

"Who then can be saved" (vv. 26-27)?

10. Peter exclaims, "We have left all we had." What does Jesus' reply say about the so-called cost of following him (vv. 29-30)?

---

11. As you consider something you may have to give up to follow Jesus, do these stories give you a sense of despair or hope? Explain.

Ask God to help you hear Jesus calling to you. Ask him to clarify the things that you need to give up to follow him. Ask him to help you to follow Jesus. He will!

Now or Later

12. Unlike his disciples, Jesus makes children a priority. What does it mean to receive the kingdom "like a little child" (v. 17)?

---

13. Go back to Jesus' words about children (vv. 15-17). What light do these stories throw on each other?

8

Jesus the Servant Leader

Mark 10:32-45

Leadership is a popular topic today. Leadership studies have tried to focus on the essence of leadership. Is leadership essentially a character trait? Does it arise out of situations that produce leadership? Is true leadership to be found in meeting the expectations and wants of followers, or in transforming their expectations and desires?

GROUP DISCUSSION. Think of a leader who motivated you to perform beyond your expectations. What characterized that person?

PERSONAL REFLECTION. Do you consider yourself a leader? Why or why not? Do others consider you a leader? What kind of leader do you want to be?

For Jesus, leadership meant service. In his words, "the Son of Man did not come to be served, but to serve, and to give his life as a ransom for many" (Mark 10:45). Knowing he was a king, he acted as a servant. This was his paradox of greatness. *Read Mark 10:32-45.*

1. What ideas do the disciples have about leadership?

What ideas does Jesus have about leadership?

2. As Jesus leads the way to Jerusalem, what impression do you get of him as a leader (vv. 32-34)?

3. How does the request of James and John seem inappropriate in light of verses 32-34?

4. What does it mean to sit at Jesus' right and left hand (v. 37)?

How might someone express a similar attitude to Jesus today?

5. How does Jesus challenge and clarify their request (vv. 38-40)?

6. Why do you think the other disciples were so indignant (v. 41)?

7. How does Jesus—both in his teaching and example—stand on its head the world's concept of greatness (vv. 42-45)?

8. What opportunities for greatness do you have at home, at work or in your church?

9. It's been said that "leadership seeks great things, and acts in small things." How does Jesus show this?

10. What attracts you to a leader like Jesus?

Ask God to help you to serve wherever you lead, even if you don't consider yourself a leader. Pray for help in following Jesus' example of service. Ask God to help you know him more, especially as you study the life of his Son.

Now or Later

Read Mark 10:46-54. Does it just happen that the story of the blind beggar follows next—or are the two stories related? Explain.

Contrast the attitude "many" had toward Bartimaeus with Jesus' attitude (vv. 46-52).

9

Jesus the Puzzling King

Mark 11

Every leader must know how to symbolize an important cause. In *Camelot* King Arthur's cause was "Might for Right." He wanted to use power for good. Up until then the practice had been "Might makes right"—those who had power could do whatever they wanted to. He symbolized his idea through the use of the Round Table, where all would have an equal hearing and equal participation, even himself, the King.

GROUP DISCUSSION. If you were doing an advertising campaign for Jesus, what symbols would you suggest he use?

PERSONAL REFLECTION. What are some common symbols of leadership and power today?

In Mark 11 we see several examples of Jesus' use of symbolism—and all of them are rather puzzling and unexpected. After many months of making people be quiet about him, Jesus goes public and provokes an outcry of acclaim. The Savior who has gently healed the sick and forgiven the sinner now curses a fig tree and causes a near riot by driving merchandisers out of the temple. Strange symbols indeed!

Yet these symbols are chosen and timed to show that Jesus comes both with meekness and judgment. The whole chapter spotlights his right to inspect his own kingdom. *Read Mark 11.*

---

1. This passage takes place over three days. Clarify the sequence of events: which events happen on which day?

---

2. What is the significance of Jesus' riding into Jerusalem on a colt (vv. 16; see Zechariah 9:9)?

---

3. What kind of king do the symbols in verses 7-11 represent?

---

4. The people shouted "Hosannah"—that is, "Save us." What kind of king and kingdom were they expecting?

---

5. In what ways has the reality of Jesus clashed with your expectations?

6. "He looked around at everything" (v. 11). What does this imply about the purpose of Jesus' visit (see Malachi 3:15)?

7. Jesus' judgment on the fig tree (vv. 12-14) seems out of character for someone who came to give life. How would you explain it?

8. How might the scene in the temple (vv. 15-17) be related to the incident of the fig tree?

9. What could "leaves without fruit" mean in our churches, our society, our personal lives?

What can we do to cultivate the kind of fruit Jesus is looking for?

10. Jesus' actions in Jerusalem provoke a discussion about his authority (vv. 27-33). Why does Jesus refuse to answer the religious leaders?

---

11. Some people would like Jesus to be their Savior and friend but not their King and Lord. What does this study say about the importance of submitting to Christ's authority?

Tell God what you resist giving over to his authority. Ask for a greater experience of his love. Knowing God's love makes submitting to him that much easier.

Now or Later

Read Mark 12:1-12 in light of chapter 11. In what sense is this story Jesus' own autobiography?

10

Jesus the Prophet

Matthew 24:1-31

The Chinese have a proverb: "Prophesying is always very difficult, especially about the future!" In the Bible, prophecy is not only knowledge of the future but insight into the present. In Matthew 24 we see Jesus as a very realistic prophet. His picture of what lies ahead is not of a world where everything will get better and better. He does not begin to suggest that everyone will eagerly embrace his cause or his followers.

GROUP DISCUSSION. Why do you think so many people are fascinated with prophecy—biblical and otherwise?

PERSONAL REFLECTION. If you could ask for a prophecy about your own life, what would you want to know about: what career to choose? who you will marry? how God will call you to serve him?

False prophets tell us what we want to hear. True prophets tell us what we need to hear. We would like Jesus to be the great positive thinker. Yet he came not only to bring peace to the troubled but trouble to those who are being lulled into a false peace. *Read Matthew 24:1-31.*

---

1. If you were a reporter assigned to cover Jesus' speech, what would be your headline?

2. The disciples asked "When?" (v. 3). Why do you think Jesus did not answer them more directly?

3. In verses 4 and 5 Jesus warns his disciples about being deceived. What are some marks of a deceiver (see Matthew 7:15-20; 1 John 4:1-6)?

4. For Jesus, history is very unstable (vv. 6-8). What signs of instability does he mention?

5. How are these signs like "the beginning of birth pains" (v. 8)?

6. What will happen to Jesus' disciples and to others as the end approaches (vv. 9-13)?

7. What does it mean for us to "stand firm" (v. 13) during difficult times?

8. When the "abomination that causes desolation" comes, what actions should believers take, and why (vv. 15-22)?

9. As Jesus' followers watch for his return during those days, how can they tell the difference between false Christs and the true Christ (vv. 23-31)?

10. How can we "keep watch" and "be ready" for Jesus?

What specifically would you like to do to be ready?

Ask God for clarity in reading the "signs of the times." Ask him to guide you to be prepared for his return. Tell him you trust him to save you from judgment in those days—whether your trust is large or little for now. A small amount of faith (trust) goes a long way in the kingdom.

Now or Later
11. *Read Matthew 24:32-51.* How can we apply the lesson of the fig tree (vv. 32-35) to the events preceding Christ's return?

12. How will the coming of Christ be like the days of Noah (vv. 36-41)?

13. What do the stories of the homeowner and the servants teach us about the Lord's return (vv. 42-51)?

11

Jesus the Sacrifice

Matthew 26:1-30

A crisis reveals what kind of people we are. Some people crumble and give up in the face of a crisis. Some people deny that the crisis exists. Some people blame others for the crisis. A few people rise up to meet the crisis, doing more than anyone else in the same position was able to do.

GROUP DISCUSSION. How do you typically respond in a crisis, and why?

PERSONAL REFLECTION. Think of what you've learned about Jesus. Have you seen him encounter crises? How did he respond?

In Matthew 26 the hostility that began early in Jesus' ministry approaches a violent end. Although he awaits his arrest and crucifixion, he is magnificently in control. *He* plans the last meal. *He* knows who will betray him. *He* offers himself as a sacrifice. When we—like Jesus—are doing the Father's will, even the inevitabilities of sin, suffering and death lose their power to imprison us. Here the victim is the one who is most free! *Read Matthew 26:1-30.*

---

1. How do you see Jesus responding to the crisis he is coming to in the four episodes you read in this passage?

2. What do these final days reveal about the character of the chief priests and elders (vv. 1-5)?

---

3. Look at verses 6-13. What factors justified the woman's extravagance?

Why is her act to be linked with the gospel (v. 13)?

---

4. What do we learn about Judas (vv. 14-16)?

---

5. What was the significance of "the Passover" (v. 17; see Exodus 12:1-29)?

---

6. What irony do you see in the disciples making preparation for Jesus to eat the Passover meal (v. 17)?

---

7. Jesus is portrayed by some as a wonderful but helpless martyr. What words and actions show him to be very much in control (vv. 18-25)?

How did he show extraordinary knowledge and insight?

8. What does verse 24 tell us about God's will and human responsibility?

9. What does the Lord's Supper teach us about the meaning of Jesus' death (vv. 26-29)?

10. What can we infer from the Lord's Supper about the kind of response we need to make in order to benefit from Jesus' death?

Ask God to guide you through a crisis you may be facing. If you can say it and mean it, tell Jesus you appreciate the crisis he faced for you, and ask him to help you to change to be more like him.

Now or Later

To some, the woman's pouring of costly perfume was a waste (vv. 6-13). To Jesus, it was beautiful. When can extravagance be beautiful?

In what ways should we be extravagant in our worship of Jesus?

12

Jesus the Dying King

John 19:16-42

At a Colorado ranch, I met a girl who told me how she came to Christ. She used to wear a cross on a chain, simply as decoration. One day another student asked her, "Why do you wear a cross? Do you know what it means?" She was taken by surprise and stuttered that she just liked crosses. But the question stayed with her and haunted her until she joined a Bible study group where she learned about Jesus and the meaning of his cross.

GROUP DISCUSSION. How is the cross sometimes used today by people who don't know what it means? How is it used by people who know what it means but may use it differently from Christians?

PERSONAL REFLECTION. What does the cross mean to you?

John R. W. Stott asks in *The Cross of Christ* why the cross emerged as the symbol of Christ. Why did the early Christians not choose a crib where he was born, or a boat where he preached, or the towels with which he washed dirty feet, or the stone rolled away from the tomb where he rose? Stott answers that while Jesus' birth and life and preaching and resurrection are all vital, it is his crucifixion that is absolutely central to knowing him.

In John 19 we see Jesus' cross as the great divider between faith and unfaith. *Read John 19:16-37.*

---

1. What stands out to you in the passage (perhaps something that you have not noticed before)?

---

2. In verses 17 and 18 John uses very few words to describe the physical act of crucifixion. Why do you think that is?

---

3. What modern symbols of execution would have a similar impact to the cross in the first century?

How would you feel about seeing Jesus executed in that way?

4. Notice the title that Pilate puts over Jesus' head on the cross (vv. 19-20). Why did he put it there if he didn't really believe it?

5. Jesus' concern for his mother is a tender, last human act (vv. 25-27). What insight does it also give us into the relationship between Jesus' earthly and spiritual families?

6. It has been said that Jesus' cry "It is finished" (v. 30) was a shout of triumph, not a cry of resignation. What had Jesus finished?

What does that mean for you and me? (See John 1:29; 17:1-4.)

7. *Read John 19:38-42.* What does the story of the burial add to the significance of Jesus' death?

8. The cross becomes the dividing line between belief and unbelief.

Who in this chapter is on the side of belief, and who is on the side of unbelief? Explain.

---

9. Who in this chapter best symbolizes where you stand right now in relation to Jesus and his cross? Why?

Ask God to help you step across the line of the cross to belief. Thank Jesus for dying on the cross to save you. Then ask for help in living your life in gratitude for his sacrifice.

Now or Later

10. The soldiers' gambling (v. 24) seems like a small detail. But here and in verses 28 and 36 John sees the crucifixion as fulfilling Old Testament Scripture. What significance does this give to Jesus' death?

---

11. Why are the incidents in verses 31-37 about not breaking Jesus' legs but piercing him with a spear important—what do they prove?

---

12. Nicodemus has appeared twice before in John's Gospel (see 3:1-12; 7:50-52). What effect does Jesus' death seem to have on him?

13

Jesus the Risen Lord

John 20

Lane Adams, a friend of mine, used to be an entertainer. Although fairly successful, he wondered why he was not happy. Along with his wife, who was also in show business, he began a spiritual search. Together they read Matthew's, Mark's and Luke's accounts of Jesus. When they got to the end of John's Gospel, they came across the story of "doubting Thomas" who told the other disciples that he certainly did not believe Jesus had risen from the dead.

"At last an honest man," exclaimed my friend. "He doesn't believe it either!" But as they continued to read, they found that Jesus appeared to the skeptical Thomas and that his doubt was turned into faith. Lane puzzled over the story and, turning to his wife, said, "I don't understand this. But I know that Jesus is alive someplace. And I mean to find him." Find him he did. And shortly thereafter my friend began a lifelong ministry of telling others about a living Christ.

GROUP DISCUSSION. Think of someone you know who has died—preferably someone you loved. How would you respond if that person suddenly walked into the room?

PERSONAL REFLECTION. What causes you to doubt that Jesus is alive? What causes you to doubt that God exists? What do you do in these times of doubt?

The resurrection is the climax of Jesus' story. If it is true, it is the most important event in history. It tells us that all that Jesus was and is and said and did and lived was true. If it is not true, then what Jesus said and did and claimed and lived is all thrown into doubt. The twentieth chapter of John's Gospel presents to us evidence, both physical and personal, that demands a decision. *Read John 20.* (If you've read it before, try to imagine this is the first time you've ever read it.)

1. What details in this passage make it seem like genuine, eyewitness testimony?

2. In verses 1-9 John records three witnesses of the empty tomb: Mary, Peter and "the other disciple." What important facts do we learn from each one?

3. John records three personal meetings with Jesus, starting with Mary (vv. 1-2, 10-18). What impresses you about her experience?

4. Jesus appears to his disciples in verses 19-23. What do they see and hear from Jesus?

---

5. Finally, Jesus appears to Thomas (vv. 24-29). For centuries he has been dubbed as "doubting Thomas." Do you think this is a fair description? Why or why not?

---

6. How does Jesus deal with Thomas's skepticism?

---

7. How does Thomas's exclamation (v. 28) provide the climax to John's Gospel?

---

8. Are you one of those who have not seen but yet have believed (v. 29)? If so, why do you believe?

If not, what do you make of this chapter?

---

9. Reread verses 30 and 31. How does John's statement help us understand the central message and urgent purpose of his Gospel?

10. What have you appreciated most about your study of Jesus these past few days or weeks?

Thank God for what you have learned about him in the course of these studies. If you believe Jesus is God's Son thank God for that faith and for the life that you have in his name.

Now or Later

11. Sometimes it is said that Jesus had a "spiritual" resurrection, not a physical one. What bits of hard evidence here support a physical resurrection?

12. What facts indicate that Jesus' body was both similar to what it was before and somewhat different (vv. 14-15, 19, 20-27)?

13. What convinced the people in this chapter that Jesus was alive again?

Leader's Notes

Leading a Bible discussion can be an enjoyable and rewarding experience. But it can also be *scary*, especially if you've never done it before. If this is your feeling, you're in good company. When God asked Moses to lead the Israelites out of Egypt, he replied, "O Lord, please send someone else to do it"! (Ex 4:13). It was the same with Solomon, Jeremiah and Timothy, but God helped these people in spite of their weaknesses, and he will help you as well.

You don't need to be an expert on the Bible or a trained teacher to lead a Bible discussion. The idea behind these inductive studies is that the leader guides group members to discover for themselves what the Bible has to say. This method of learning will allow group members to remember much more of what is said than a lecture would.

These studies are designed to be led easily. As a matter of fact, the flow of questions through the passage, from observation to interpretation to application, is so natural that you may feel the studies lead themselves. This study guide is also flexible. You can use it with a variety of groups— student, professional, neighbourhood or church groups. Each study takes forty-five to sixty minutes in a group setting.

There are some important facts to know about group dynamics and encouraging discussion. The suggestions listed below should enable you to fulfil your role as leader effectively and enjoyably.

Preparing for the Study

1. Ask God to help you understand and apply the passage in your own life. Unless this happens, you will not be prepared to lead others. Pray too for the various members of the group. Ask God to open your hearts

to the message of his Word and motivate you to action.

2. Read the introduction to the guide to get an overview of the entire book and the issues that will be explored.

3. As you begin each study, read and reread the assigned Bible passage to familiarize yourself with it.

4. This study guide is based on the New International Version of the Bible. It will help you and the group if you use this translation as the basis for your study and discussion.

5. Carefully work through each question in the study. Spend time in meditation and reflection as you consider how to respond.

6. Write your thoughts and responses in the space provided in the study guide. This will help you to express your understanding of the passage clearly.

7. It might help to have a Bible dictionary handy. Use it to look up any unfamiliar words, names or places. (For additional help on how to study a passage, see chapter five of *How to lead a Lifeguide Bible Study*, IVP).

8. Consider how you can apply the Scripture to your life. Remember that the group will follow your lead in responding to the studies. They will not go any deeper than you do.

9. Once you have finished your own study of the passage, familiarize yourself with the leader's notes for the study you are leading. These are designed to help you in several ways. First, they tell you the purpose the study guide author had in mind when writing the study. Take time to think through how the study questions work together to accomplish that purpose. Second, the notes provide you with additional background information or suggestions on group dynamics for various questions. This information can be useful when people have difficulty understanding or answering a question. Third, the leader's notes can alert you to potential problems you may encounter during the study.

10. If you wish to remind yourself of anything mentioned in the leader's notes, make a note to yourself below that question in the study.

Leading the Study

1. Begin the study on time. Open with prayer, asking God to help the group understand and apply the passage.

2. Be sure that everyone in your group has a study guide. Encourage

the group to prepare beforehand for each discussion by reading the introduction to the guide and by working through the questions in the study.

3. At the beginning of your first time together, explain that these studies are meant to be discussions, not lectures. Encourage the members of
the group to participate. However, do not put pressure on those who may
be hesitant to speak during the first few sessions. You may want to suggest the following guidelines to your group.

■ Stick to the topic being discussed.

■ Your responses should be based on the verses which are the focus of
the discussion and not on outside authorities such as commentaries or
speakers.

■ These studies focus on a particular passage of Scripture. Only rarely
should you refer to other portions of the Bible. This allows for everyone
to participate in in-depth study on equal ground.

■ Anything said in the group is considered confidential and will not be
discussed outside the group unless specific permission is given to do so.

■ We will listen attentively to each other and provide time for each person present to talk.

■ We will pray for each other.

4. Have a group member read the introduction at the beginning of the
discussion.

5. Every session begins with a group discussion question. The question or activity is meant to be used before the passage is read. The question introduces the theme of the study and encourages group members to
begin to open up. Encourage as many members as possible to participate,
and be ready to get the discussion going with your own response.

This section is designed to reveal where our thoughts or feelings need
to be transformed by Scripture. That is why it is especially important not
to read the passage before the discussion question is asked. The passage
will tend to color the honest reactions people would otherwise give
because they are, of course, supposed to think the way the Bible does.

You may want to supplement the group discussion question with an
icebreaker to help people to get comfortable. For more ideas, see Appen-
dix A of *The Small-Group Leader* by John Mallison (Scripture Union).

You also might want to use the personal reflection question with your
group. Either allow a time of silence for people to respond individually or

discuss it together.

6. Have a group member (or members if the passage is long) read aloud the passage to be studied. Then give people several minutes to read the passage again silently so that they can take it all in.

7. Question 1 will generally be an overview question designed to briefly survey the passage. Encourage the group to look at the whole passage, but try to avoid getting sidetracked by questions or issues that will be addressed later in the study.

8. As you ask the questions, keep in mind that they are designed to be used just as they are written. You may simply read them aloud, or you may prefer to express them in your own words.

There may be times when it is appropriate to deviate from the study guide. For example, a question may have already been answered. If so, move on to the next. Or someone may raise an important question not covered in the guide. Take time to discuss it, but try to keep the group from going off at a tangent.

9. Avoid answering your own questions. If necessary, repeat or rephrase them until they are clearly understood, or point out something you have read in the leader's notes to clarify the context or meaning. An eager group quickly becomes passive and silent if they think the leader will do most of the talking.

10. Don't be afraid of silence. People may need time to think about the question before formulating their answers.

11. Don't be content with just one answer. Ask, "What do the rest of you think?" or "Anything else?" until several people have given answers to the question.

12. Acknowledge all contributions. Try to be affirming whenever possible. Never reject an answer. If it is clearly off-base, ask, "Which verse led you to that conclusion?" or again, "What do the rest of you think?"

13. Don't expect every answer to be addressed to you, even though this will probably happen at first. As group members become more at ease, they will begin to truly interact with each other. This is one sign of healthy discussion.

14. Don't be afraid of controversy. It can be very stimulating. If you don't resolve an issue completely, don't be frustrated. Move on and keep it in mind for later. A subsequent study may solve the problem.

15. Periodically summarize what the group has said about the passage. This helps to draw together the various ideas mentioned and gives continuity to the study. But don't preach.

16. At the end of the Bible discussion you may want to allow group members a time of quiet to work on an idea under "Now or Later." Then discuss what you experienced. Or you may want to encourage group members to work on these ideas between meetings. Give an opportunity during the session for people to talk about what they are learning.

17. Conclude your time together with conversational prayer, adapting the prayer suggestion at the end of the study to your group. Ask for God's help in following through on the commitments you've made.

18. End on time.

Many more suggestions and helps are found in *How to lead a Lifeguide Bible Study,* (InterVarsity Press, US).

Components of Small Groups

A healthy small group should do more than study the Bible. There are four components to consider as you structure your time together.

Nurture. Small groups help us to grow in our knowledge and love of God. Bible study is the key to making this happen and is the foundation of your small group.

Community. Small groups are a great place to develop deep friendships with other Christians. Allow time for informal interaction before and after each study. Plan activities and games that will help you get to know each other. Spend time having fun—going on a picnic or cooking dinner together.

Worship and prayer. Your study will be enhanced by spending time praising God together in prayer or song. Pray for each other's needs, and keep track of how God is answering prayer in your group. Ask God to help you apply what you are learning in your study.

Outreach. Reaching out to others can be a practical way of applying what you are learning, and it will keep your group from becoming self-focused. Host a series of evangelistic discussions for your friends or neighbors. Clean up the yard of an elderly friend. Serve at a soup kitchen together, or spend a day working on a Habitat house.

Many more suggestions and helps in each of these areas are found in

The Small-Group Leader. Information on building a small group can be found there and in *Small Group Starter Kit* (Scripture Union), *Small Group Leaders' Handbook* and *The Big Book on Small Groups* (both from InterVarsity Press). Reading through one of these books would be worth your time.

Study 1. The Real Jesus. Mark 1:9-45.

Purpose: To see how Jesus was identified and introduced to the people of his time.

Group discussion. These questions are important for several reasons. First, they help the group to warm up to each other. No matter how well a group may know each other, there is always a stiffness that needs to be overcome before people will begin to talk openly. Second, they get people thinking along the lines of the topic of the study. Most people will have lots of different things going on in their minds (dinner, an important meeting coming up, how to get the car fixed) that will have nothing to do with the study. A creative question will get their attention and draw them into the discussion. Third, they can reveal where our thoughts or feelings need to be transformed by Scripture. This is why it is especially important not to read the passage before the question is asked. The passage will tend to color the honest reactions people would otherwise give because they are, of course, supposed to think the way the Bible does.

Question 2. This may be a difficult question for some, so give the group time to think. If they still need help, you might mention that baptism was an act of "repentance for the forgiveness of sins" (v. 4). Because Jesus was sinless, he had no personal need for repentance. Yet he submitted to baptism both as an example to others and as a way of identifying with sinful Israel. Having identified himself with those deserving God's judgment, he later experienced that judgment on their behalf when he died on the cross. Jesus' temptation brings to mind two previous temptations, those involving Adam and Israel in the wilderness. Concerning the latter, Moses wrote, "the LORD your God . . . led you through the vast and dreadful desert . . . to humble you and to test you" (Deut 8:14-16). Both Adam and Israel failed the test, but Jesus proved himself to be the true Son of God and the new Israel by resisting the temptation.

Question 4. Some background information might help the group with this question. Throughout their history the Israelites looked forward to the coming of the kingdom of God (see Is 9:7; Dan 2:44; 7:18, 22, 27). However, by the time of Jesus they believed the kingdom would be earthly and political. They thought the Messiah would come and overthrow the Romans, who had conquered Israel. So although Jesus' words "the kingdom of God is near" would be viewed as good news, that news was misinterpreted by the people. Biblically speaking, the "kingdom of God" (v. 15) refers not to a territory or political system, but to the dynamic reign of God which had come to a decisive point with the coming of Jesus.

Question 5. This was not the first time Simon and Andrew had met Jesus (see Jn 1:35-42; see also Lk 5:1-11).

Question 7. The Bible frequently refers to demons or "evil spirits" (vv. 23-27, 32). Some have tried to explain such references as primitive attempts to account for mental or physical illness. However, the Bible provides its own explanation. Evil spirits are fallen angels who are led by Satan, the prince of demons, in an attempt to thwart the work of God in the world. Both the devil and evil spirits were finally defeated by Jesus Christ on the cross and will be cast into eternal fire after his return (Col 2:15; Mt 25:41).

Question 9. The Greek word here translated as "leprosy" was used for various diseases affecting the skin—not just for leprosy. Those with "leprosy" were outcasts, who were forced to live outside the community. They were required to shout "Unclean, unclean!" whenever they approached a group of people. Theirs was a tragic and lonely existence. "But go, show yourself to the priest . . . as a testimony to them" (vv. 43-44). Jesus' miracles were not just wonderworks. They were pointers and signs to who he was.

Question 10. In his early days Jesus did not want people to misunderstand the kind of Messiah that he was—a healer or a wonderworker rather than a Savior. Later he spoke freely and ordered his disciples to speak freely.

Prayer. Generally speaking, prayer is something that believers do. However, anyone can speak to God. If you are leading a group that includes seekers, you can make these prayer times accessible to them. Assure them they don't have to say anything they don't want to. Encourage them to pray silently if they like, or out loud. Model simple prayers like the ones given in these studies. All of these things should help the prayer time to be a good application time for everyone in your study, both seekers and believers.

Now or Later. If time allows for this question, you may want to insert it after question 10 and include it in your response to questions 11-12.

"Son of God" (v. 1) is a theme repeated at Jesus' baptism (1:11), transfiguration (9:7) and death (15:39). It's a thread that weaves through Mark. Mark's opening words about Jesus the Son of God remind us that the early Christians had the fish as a symbol of Jesus. The letters of the word *fish* in Greek—ICHTHUS—are the first letters of "Jesus Christ, Son of God, Saviour."

Study 2. The Surprising Jesus. Luke 5:17-32.
Purpose: To gain a fresh look at Jesus that may be different than what we expect.

Question 1. The Pharisees and teachers of the law were conspicuous on this occasion. Who were they? The Pharisees ("separated ones") were a group of Jews who banded together to preserve the purity of their faith. Although the Pharisees included some priests, most of them were laypersons, such as craftsmen, farmers and merchants. They were extremely conscious of ritual and cleanliness, and they interpreted the law in a legalistic and oppressive manner.

The teachers of the law, scribes, were originally people who wrote documents and kept records. They often held high administrative positions. By the time of Jesus they had also become teachers and experts in the law of Moses. They were called on to give legal and theological opinions and often had a group of disciples who followed them wherever they went.

Question 4. "Which is easier" (v. 23)—Obviously it was easier to say "be forgiven." No one could see the forgiveness of sins. But everyone could see if the man actually got up and walked.

Question 5. Note that Levi is also called Matthew in the Bible. The *Handbook of Life in Bible Times* gives us insights into tax collectors such as Levi: "Taxation was heavy for the people of Judea at the time, which explains why tax collectors were among the most despised of people, not least because they were Jews working for the hated Romans. Tax collectors paid a fee to the authorities which covered the tax and allowed them an adequate reward for their work. But they extracted far more than was reasonable from the people and made a handsome profit" (J. A. Thompson, InterVarsity Press, 1986, p. 225).

Questions 6-8. Jesus was a friend of sinners. He came to heal them, not to leave them sick. Doctors are for sick people, but they do not approve of disease. In the same way, Jesus is for sinners but not for sin. He couldn't be true to his call and avoid sinners. But sinners couldn't become his friends and remain unchanged.

Question 11. According to the Mosaic law, fasting was only required on the Day of Atonement (Lev 16:29, 31; 23:27-32; Num 29:7). Four other fasts were observed by the Jews after the Babylonian exile (Zech 7:5; 8:19). However, by the time of Jesus the Pharisees fasted twice a week (Lk 18:12).

In response to the Pharisees' question about fasting, Jesus compares himself to a bridegroom (vv. 34-35). Jewish weddings were times of joyous celebration where fasting, a sign of mourning, would be inappropriate. Jesus does say, however, that when he is "taken from them" (perhaps a reference to his death) it will be appropriate to fast.

Question 12. The old garments and wine skins were the traditions of rabbinic Judaism, traditions that fossilized into ironclad rules and systems that squeezed out life and joy.

Study 3. Jesus the Storytelling Teacher. Mark 4:1-25.
Purpose: To understand why it is important to practice the truth we know.
Question 2. A parable is a story designed to elicit a *response* from the hearer. Usually the story relates to things which are familiar to the audience such as seed, soils, lamps, plants, birds and so on. However, parables often take an unexpected twist, leading to a conclusion that is different or even opposite from what the audience anticipated. For example, in the Parable of the Good Samaritan the audience would have expected the religious men (the priest and Levite) to stop and help the man on the side of the road. The *last* person they would have expected to stop was a despised Samaritan. This unexpected twist in the story caught the audience off guard and forced them to reevaluate their definition of "neighbor." The Parable of the Sower lacks this element of surprise, but it

invites the immediate response of "What kind of soil am I?"

Question 4. The seed is the word, the path stands for hardness, the rocky places for shallowness, the thorns for the worries and desires of this life, and the good soil for receptiveness. Similarly, the birds stand for Satan and the sun for trouble.

Question 5. "Ears to hear"—Note verses 3, 9, 12, 15, 16, 18, 20, 23 and 24 as instances of the recurring theme "Let him *hear.*"

Question 7. Concerning "the secret of the kingdom" (v. 11), R. V. G. Tasker writes:

> Matthew makes it clear . . . as the other evangelists do not, that Jesus deliberately adopted the parabolic method at a particular stage in His ministry for the purpose of withholding further truth about Himself and the kingdom of heaven from the crowds, who had proved themselves deaf to His claims and irresponsive to His demands. . . . Hitherto He had used parables as illustrations . . . now when addressing the unbelieving multitudes, He speaks only in parables, which He interprets to his disciples in private. . . . There were mysteries (secrets) of the kingdom . . . which could not be understood by those who . . . looked upon him with their eyes but never understood the significance of his person. (*The Gospel According to St. Matthew*, Tyndale New Testament Commentaries, IVP, 1961, pp. 134-35.)

In my opinion Jesus used parables both as a judgment of those who would not hear and as mercy on those who were not ready to hear. Another way to put it is that a parable may light up a truth, may lead on to further truth or may let down those who are not ready for truth. To "hear the word, accept it, and produce a crop" (v. 20) could be put: "let it in, let it root, and let it grow."

Question 9. In verses 24-25 we see the law of growth and loss, or "use it or lose it." Jesus' teaching is that there will either be spiritual growth or atrophy. The parables do not deliberately obscure the truth. That would not make any more sense than lighting a lamp and hiding it. The ultimate purpose of a parable is to reveal truth, not to conceal it. Whether we "use it or lose it" will depend on how we hear.

Question 11. The mustard seed is not the smallest seed known today. Some have claimed, therefore, that Jesus is guilty of making an inaccurate statement. However, this is to demand a verbal precision that goes beyond the purpose of his words. The mustard seed was the smallest seed used by Palestinian farmers and gardeners. To that audience his statement would be both clear and accurate.

"The largest of all garden plants" (v. 32): Under the right conditions, the mustard plant could reach a height of ten feet.

The birds of the air can perch in its shade" (v. 32): The birds are probably a symbol of the Gentiles or nations who will come to Christ. (See Dan 4:20-22 for a similar reference.)

Study 4. Jesus the Master over Fear. Luke 8:22-39.

Purpose: To identify our fears and let Jesus deal with them.

Question 1. Note that both of these stories happened by the lake. In the Old and New Testaments, lakes and seas are taken both as places of danger and threat and places where God displays his power. The God who led the people of Israel through the Red Sea now makes a path over the lake for Jesus' followers.

Squalls come up very quickly on the Lake of Galilee (v. 23). Church fathers like Tertullian saw a parable here—the "little ship" of the church rocked in the storm of opposition.

Question 3. The best way to counter our questioning and doubts is to face Jesus' questions and demands. His questions often expose the reasons for our doubts. We live in an age of skepticism, an age in which people question everything. We forget that God is also questioning us!

Question 4. Notice also the question "Who is this?" in verse 25. The fear of the storm gives way to a much deeper terror or sense of awe over Jesus. Our spiritual constancy depends not so much on our inner courage or positive circumstances as our growing trust in the person of Christ.

Question 5. Note how evil makes people like this man dwell "in the tombs" (v. 27)—in a living death, whether of personality kinks or antisocial behavior. Here is a living demonstration of how evil isolates, binds and leads to self-destructive behavior.

William L. Lane comments on "the region of the Gerasenes" (v. 26):

> The point of arrival is indicated in a general way as the district of the Gerasenes, most probably in reference to a town whose name is preserved in the modern Kersa or Koursi. At the site of Kersa the shore is level, and there are

no tombs. But about a mile further south there is a fairly steep slope within forty yards from the shore, and about two miles from there cavern tombs are found which appear to have been used for dwellings. (*The Gospel According to Mark*, The New International Commentary on the New Testament, Eerdmans, 1974, p. 181.)

The "similar reactions" you should discuss are those people have today when confronted by something good but unusual or frightening. For example, the kind of reaction people might have if someone evil suddenly becomes a Christian and changes overnight.

Question 6. Again Jesus counters a question with a question (v. 30). He asked the man a question, but the demons replied, showing that they were in control. Jesus makes the spirits come into the open in order to be identified, to take off their mask, so to speak.

"'Legion,' he replied, because many demons had gone into him" (v. 30). A Roman legion consisted of six thousand men. This man's soul, or person, had become enemy-occupied territory.

The presence of pigs (v. 32) indicates that this was Gentile territory, because these animals were unclean to the Jews, who would never have kept them.

"He gave them permission" to go into the pigs (vv. 32-33). Why didn't he totally destroy the demons? Perhaps (1) a visible demonstration was needed that the power of God was really stronger or (2) at this stage of the battle with evil, the Lord still allowed evil some territory. In missionary situations today there is often a "power encounter" where the living power of Jesus Christ is demonstrated in a tangible way over fear, sickness and evil spirits, and results in the freeing and conversion of an entire tribal group.

Question 7. Note the contrast between verses 37 and 38. The people ask Jesus to go. The man begs to go with Jesus.

Question 8. Verse 39 presents a mini-missionary challenge: The man's request to go with Jesus is refused, his place of service is set out and the theme of his testimony is assigned to him.

Question 11. The woman's hemorrhage would have made her ceremonially unclean and would have made her a social outcast, since anyone touching her would also become unclean (Lev 15:25-27). Her desperation is seen by the fact that she enters the crowd anyway and touches Jesus.

Why does she come from behind and why just touch him (v. 44)? She didn't dare appear openly. The woman is a touching mixture of superstition, faith, disappointment and hope.

"Power has gone out" (v. 46)—like the positive and negative poles of a battery, the healings were not without cost, not least because our physical diseases are partly related to the battle with sin.

Note the contrast of two kinds of contact—the casual touch of the jostling crowd (v. 45) and the intentional touch of the woman (v. 46). Why does Jesus make her show herself (vv. 45-48)? Faith is called not only to believe but to confess. To speak at all as a woman before an Eastern crowd and with her sickness was very humbling.

Question 12. The delay allowed the faith of the father to be tested. He believed in spite of a deadly illness, a delay, a disappointment and mockery.

Question 13. "She is not dead but asleep" (v. 52). It is not certain whether the child was in a coma or really dead. Jesus may have been using *sleep* as a metaphor of death—a sleep that is conquered for the believer by Christ.

"Give her something to eat" (v. 55). Notice how practical Jesus is. He doesn't expect us to live on a daily ration of miracles.

Study 5. Jesus the Challenging Saviour. Mark 8:22-38.
Purpose: To understand the place of the cross in Jesus' ministry and in our lives.

Questions 1-4. There are at least three unusual features about this healing: (1) Jesus led the blind man outside the village, (2) he spit on the man's eyes, and (3) the man was healed in two stages.

This story of a "second touch" is placed beautifully between a previous question to the disciples, "Do you still not understand?" (v. 21), and the confession "You are the Christ" (8:29). Their first days with Jesus had given some sight, as with the blind man. The second touch would give them clear sight as to who Jesus was.

Today we often think of a second touch in terms of a "second blessing, "but Mark puts it in terms of Jesus' suffering and of the cost of discipleship. Jesus tried to keep his healings secret (v. 26) since those uninterested in salvation might have tried to misuse him. "Miracles were not his major work but byproducts of his living power. . . . What good was sight without something worth seeing" (David Redding, *The Miracles and the Parables*, Fleming H. Revell, 1971, p. 96).

Question 2. John was a stern prophet of doom. Elijah was a wonderworker. All the prophets embodied partial truths that converged in the full truth of Jesus.

Question 6. What a stern rebuke to Peter! Satan had tempted Jesus to be the wrong kind of Messiah at the very beginning (see Mk 1:12 and the expanded accounts of the temptation in, for example, Mt 4:1-11). Now Satan at this second stage comes in a different guise—in the confessing disciple Peter—seeking to divert Jesus from the redemptive work of the cross.

Question 7. Here we see the illuminating work of God. He touched the blind man's eyes twice, and he needed to touch the disciples' spiritual eyes twice. Most of the people around had closed eyes—they saw Jesus only as another prophet. Peter and then the other disciples had their eyes opened to see that Jesus was the Messiah. But they still needed a second touch to see what kind of Messiah he was—a suffering, dying Savior.

For Jesus, suffering had to come before glory, and the same is true today. Yet many Christians wrongly assume—as Peter did—that we can have the latter without the former.

Question 8. "Take up his cross" (v. 34). In the first century the cross was an instrument of death, and those who took up a cross were on the way to their execution. Jesus took up the cross of salvation as a sinbearer. We who are sinners cannot do that. Ours is a cross of witness and service, putting self aside for the sake of Christ and the gospel.

"For me and for the gospel" (v. 35). A Christian who follows Jesus has two crosses: Christ and the gospel. "For Christ" keeps our commitment personal. "For the gospel" keeps it specific. Keeping both together will save us from mere activism on the one hand or mere sentimentality on the other.

Now or Later. "He then began to teach them" (v. 31). Here begins stage two of Jesus' teaching of who the Messiah is and why he comes. Up until now he had not spoken of his suffering, cross, resurrection and return. From now on he will be telling and living the rest of the story (see 10:32-34 for an example).

This question may be difficult for some, since it cannot be answered directly from the passage. If the group has difficulty, you might ask: "Why couldn't Jesus simply have entered Jerusalem and set up his kingdom—as his disciples expected? Why did the cross have to come first?"

Study 6. Jesus the Source of Power. Mark 9:2-32.

Purpose: To take hold of the promise that "everything is possible for him who believes."

Question 2. "Transfigured" (v. 2), literally = *metamorphosed*, a word we use to describe a radical transformation (for example, from a caterpillar to a butterfly). This same word is used in Romans 12:2 and 2 Corinthians 3:18 to describe the transformation of Christians by the Holy Spirit.

"A cloud appeared" (v. 7)—as at Sinai, where God gave the law. A voice said, "This is my Son," as at Jesus' baptism (1:11).

"Jesus gave them orders not to tell anyone" (v. 9). His pattern of reserving revelation continues. His death and resurrection are crucial to understanding him, but his followers still don't understand it. It's obvious that they also do not understand nor expect his eventual resurrection (v. 10).

The disciples' question about Elijah (v. 11) shows they did accept Jesus as Messiah but were puzzled. Elijah was supposed to come first. Well, where was he? Jesus replied, "Elijah has come" (v. 13), referring to John the Baptist.

Question 3. The transfiguration occurred shortly after Jesus had announced his death (see Mk 8:31-32). The disciples had expected Jesus to inaugurate the kingdom when he reached Jerusalem, but instead he told them he would be crucified. They needed to be encouraged that the kingdom would eventually come in power and in glory, and the transfiguration gave them (and us) a glimpse of that wonderful event. We too need to be encouraged that the kingdom will eventually come, especially since we have been waiting for it for nearly two thousand years. It might help the group to read Peter's statements about the transfiguration in 2 Peter 1:16-18.

Question 5. If the group is slow to respond, suggest three possibilities—the teachers, the crowd, the father or the disciples. The teachers showed stubborn unbelief, the disciples showed prayerless unbelief, the father showed seeking unbelief.

Question 8. Verse 31 is Jesus' third prediction of his passion (see 8:31; 9:12). But the disciples are still too dense to understand. This underlines that the cross is the heart of Christianity and also the hardest thing to accept and understand.

Question 11. It is easy to see why the boy's father would have been discouraged. He had brought his son to Jesus' disciples, but they had been unable to help. By the time Jesus arrived on the scene, the father could only say, "if you can"—for he wasn't sure Jesus could do anything either.

William Barclay comments about the disciples: "They have been equipped with power but needed prayer to keep and to maintain that power" (*The Gospel of Mark*, St. Andrew's Press, 1964, p. 225).

Study 7. Jesus & a Rich Man. Luke 18:15-30.

Purpose: To realize that Jesus must be the number one priority in our lives.

Question 2. Wrong assumption 1: Jesus is just a teacher. Wrong assumption 2: We can do something to merit eternal life.

Question 3. Jesus' words have two possible interpretations. One is that he is claiming he is not God and so does not deserve to be called good. The second is that he is good and therefore deserves to be viewed and obeyed as God, not just as a "good teacher."

Questions 4-6. The Ten Commandments divide naturally into two parts. The first part (four commandments) describe our relation to God (Ex 20:1-11), the second part (six commandments) our relation to others (vv. 12-17). When Jesus lists the Ten Commandments, he leaves out the first part and mentions only five commands in the second part, omitting the final command about coveting. Why?

The rich man had lived a decent life humanly speaking, keeping the commands about adultery, murder, stealing and false testimony—at least outwardly. However, when Jesus asked him to "sell everything you have" his weak spot was exposed. He was covetous and therefore had broken not only the tenth commandment but also the first two, which forbid idolatry (see Col 3:5). Money had become his god, and he was unwilling to give it up to follow Jesus.

According to Mark 10:21, Jesus looked at the man and loved him. But

Jesus loved him not in a way that was convenient and easy but in a way that was highest and best. He could not compromise and be true to the kingdom. Yet he loved this man enough to tell him the truth—"one thing you lack"—and to give him the chance not only of a lifetime but of eternity. This is the only man in the whole New Testament who the Bible says went away sad from Jesus.

Question 7. This question goes pretty deep. Be ready to give your response to this to get things started. It may also help to suggest common traps such as work and money.

Question 8. The camel was the largest animal found in Palestine. Jesus is using a preposterous hyperbole, referring to a huge animal going through the eye of a needle. It is a metaphor of sheer impossibility.

The interpretation that the word *camel* should actually be *rope*, because the words are similar in Greek, is unlikely. Likewise, the notion that the needle's eye was a gate by that name in Jerusalem has no evidence to support it.

The notion that rich people have great difficulty entering the kingdom astounded those listening to Jesus (see v. 26). Popular theology of that day claimed that riches were God's reward for right living. Therefore, it was assumed that the rich would have the easiest time entering the kingdom.

Question 9. "What is impossible with men is possible with God" (v. 27): Salvation, as clearly taught here, is never a human achievement for anyone—including the rich man. Why? Because salvation is based on what Christ has done for us on the cross, not on what we think we can do for God.

Question 11. It has been said that grace is all of Christ for all of us, and faith involves all of us for all of Christ. A good summary of this passage!

Question 12. What marks a childlike attitude? Humility, openness, trust, dependency, helplessness—and what other qualities?

We still make the mistake of the disciples and imagine we have more important things to do than spend time on children (v. 15). But kingdom seekers should have time to be child receivers.

We talk a lot about "receiving Christ" these days and, of course, rightly so. But Jesus spoke about receiving "the kingdom" (v. 17). It might help the group to think about how the two are related.

Question 13. The rich ruler had a self-righteous attitude rather than the kind of dependence and trust which is characteristic of children.

Study 8. Jesus the Servant Leader. Mark 10:32-45.
Purpose: To realize that true greatness does not mean having many servants but rather serving many.
Question 2. This is the fourth prediction of Jesus' death. Note the specific details he adds—he will be betrayed, condemned, handed over to the Gentiles, mocked, spat at and flogged. John Stott says, "Jesus was not looking *back* at a mission he had completed; . . . he was still looking *forward* to a mission which he was about to fulfil." And "he did not regard the death he was about to die as bringing his mission to an untimely end, but as actually necessary to accomplish it" (*The Cross of Christ*, InterVarsity Press,1986, pp. 67, 66).
Question 3. In Matthew 20:20-22 we discover that their mother put them up to it. A Japanese pastor friend of mine once said that a Japanese person would never have made so bold a request unless pushed by his mother!
Question 4. In Jesus' culture the seats on the right and left hand of a host or ruler were the positions of greatest honor and power. Considering that James, John and Peter were already in Jesus' inner circle, were they trying to get these two special places before Peter did, since there could be only two seated next to Jesus?
Question 5. If you don't get into the idea of sharing Jesus' "cup" and "baptism," you might ask: What does Jesus mean in verses 38 and 39 by his "cup" and his "baptism" (see Mt 26:39; Rom 6:34)?
Cup is an Old Testament symbol for suffering (see Is 51:17).The image of baptism is parallel to that of the cup and refers to Jesus' suffering and death.
Why did Jesus not have the authority to give these places? Alan Cole comments: "Even the Son is in loving subjection to His Father; it is not even for Christ to dispense honours at his will" (*The Gospel According to Mark*, Tyndale New Testament Commentaries, ed. R. V. G. Tasker, IVP, 1961, p. 170).
Question 7. The whole concept of leadership and greatness changed when Christ the Lord stooped down as a servant. In their desire for great-

ness, people are clamoring for positions at the top, where the competition is fierce. Yet according to Jesus, the true path to greatness lies at the bottom ("whoever wants to be first must be slave of all"), where there is very little competition! In his life and death Jesus modeled the kind of servant leadership he desires in us.

"A ransom" (v. 45) was the price paid to free someone from bondage. Jesus' death was the price paid to free us from our bondage to sin and death. This verse combines many Old Testament pictures: the "Son of Man" of the Psalms, Ezekiel and Daniel; the "servant" of Isaiah; the ransom idea of Psalm 49:7; and the redeeming of "the many" of Isaiah 53:11-12.

Question 9. "Leadership seeks great things"—not for itself but for others.

Study 9. Jesus the Puzzling King. Mark 11.
Purpose: To allow the reality of Jesus to reshape our image of him.
General note. Jesus' mission to serve, as taught and illustrated in chapter 10, is now balanced by chapter 11, as his authority is set forth and questioned. Symbolic acts within the chapters tie them together. True leadership is a balance of serving and ruling. Authority without humility is self-serving, while humility without authority is self-defeating.
Question 3. Jesus was riding on an ass in a procession of poverty, as shown by the scattering of clothes and the broken branches of the trees. This so-called triumphal entry (vv. 7-11) has also been called "the march of the meek one." G. Campbell Morgan commented that Jesus came in "the majesty of meekness, stripped of all those things which men usually associate with royalty" (*The Gospel According to Mark*, Living Spring Publications, reprint 1984, p. 255).
Question 4. See Psalm 118:25-27. Many Jews of Jesus' day looked for the Messiah to come as a military conqueror who would overthrow the Romans and establish Israel as the chief nation on earth.
Question 6. Malachi 3:15 indicates that the Lord would appear in the temple to inspect and judge Israel. He came looking for fruit but did not find any, as Mark 11:12-21 makes clear.

Bethany (v. 11) was the nearby home of Jesus' friends Lazarus, Martha and Mary.
Questions 7-8. If it was not the season for figs, why was Jesus so disap-

pointed not to find them? Was this an arbitrary, irrational act? Alan Cole states that "presumably the Lord was looking for the small early ripe figs, that ripen with the leaves, before the main crop" (*Mark*, p. 177).

G. Campbell Morgan comments on this unusual incident: "This is admittedly a strange story. . . . Cursing and destruction were not the usual methods of Jesus. . . . Therein is one of the chief values of this story." Isaiah had prophesied that "Jehovah will rise up . . . that he may do his work, his strange work, and bring to pass his act, his strange act." Again, Morgan comments: "When in the divine economy judgment becomes punishment . . . it is nevertheless God's strange work, his strange act" (*Mark*, p. 251). This "strange" work of Jesus shows the judgment of God on a system which has become fruitless because it is faithless. It also shows that judgment is not arbitrary. It reveals destruction and withering as much as it *imposes* it.

Question 9. If time allows, you might want to follow these questions with a couple more on the fig tree. Peter was surprised that the fig tree Jesus had cursed had actually withered (vv. 20-21). How does Jesus use this occasion to teach his disciples about faith (vv. 22-25)? How can Jesus' teaching encourage us to pray for the seemingly impossible?

On their way to Jerusalem, Jesus and his disciples would have passed through the town of Bethphage ("house of figs") on the slopes of the Mount of Olives which overlooks the Dead Sea. Jesus uses these literal objects (fig tree, mountain and the sea) to teach a spiritual lesson about faith.

Verses 22-25 require some thought. Fruitfulness is intimately related to faith, and faith is expressed in prayer. Yet both our prayers and our fruitfulness will be hindered if we are unwilling to forgive others.

Alan Cole comments on these verses: "Like tree, like temple, like nation: the parallel is exact" (*Mark*, p. 177). The fruitless fig tree evidently stands for a fruitless temple and nation. And it is fruitless because it is prayerless. The "house of prayer" is now a den of robbers.

Study 10. Jesus the Prophet. Matthew 24:1-31.
Purpose: To consider the events preceding Christ's return and the importance of being ready for him.
Overview. In this chapter Jesus warns his followers of five dangers or dif-

ficulties they will face: (1) dependence on outward structures and systems such as the temple (vv. 1-2), (2) deception by false prophets (vv. 4-5, 11, 23-26), (3) distraction by turmoil in the world (vv. 6-8), (4) dismay over persecution (vv. 9-13), and (5) dullness or apathy because of not knowing the day or hour of his return (vv. 36-51).

Each warning is accompanied by a promise: The temple may be destroyed, but the elect will be saved (v. 22); false prophets may appear, but the true Son of Man will come with the angels and be recognized (vv. 30-31); nations be in turmoil, but these are the birth pangs of a new creation (v. 8); believers may be persecuted, but the faithful will be saved (v. 13); the day of his return may not be dated, but the owner will come (vv. 42-51).

Group discussion. If you are leading a group, you may also want to ask the personal reflection question. It should lead to interesting discussion.

Question 1. Jesus' prophecy in this chapter was prompted by the disciples' fascination with the temple in Jerusalem. It was an architectural wonder and was one of the most impressive sights in the ancient world. The rabbis said, "He who has not seen the temple in its full construction has never seen a glorious building in his life." According to Josephus, the stones of the temple were white, and some of them were thirty-seven feet long, twelve feet high and eighteen feet wide. Construction of the temple was begun by Herod the Great in 20-19 B.C. and was not fully completed until six years before the temple's destruction in A.D. 70. At that time the Roman armies under Titus actually pried the stones apart to get the gold leaf that had melted from the roof during the fire. Jesus' prophecy in verse 2 was therefore literally fulfilled. For the Jews the temple was not only a great and historic building but was an assurance that God was with them. It gave them a false sense of security.

Question 4. Notice that these things are not the end (v. 6) but merely "the beginning of birth pains" (v. 8). These events will mark all of time from Jesus' first to second coming. Like birth pains, they will initially be less intense and further apart. However, as the end approaches they will increase in frequency and intensity until they culminate in the time of "great distress, unequaled from the beginning of the world until now—and never to be equaled again" (v. 21).

Question 8. Because of the difficulty of understanding the meaning of the phrase "abomination that causes desolation" spoken of by Daniel, this study does not try to unravel its meaning. However, if the subject comes up in the study you might suggest the following. Many scholars believe Daniel's prophecy was fulfilled in 168 B.C. when Antiochus Epiphanes erected a pagan altar to Zeus in the Jerusalem temple. Jesus' statement indicates, however, that there will be a future fulfilment of this prophecy as well. Some believe this fulfilment came with the Roman sacrilege of the temple during the destruction of Jerusalem in A.D. 70. Others think it will be fulfilled by the sacrilege of the antichrist at the end of time (2 Thess 2:4). Perhaps both are intended.

To understand the prophecy in this chapter, we need to know something about the so-called prophetic perspective. The Old Testament prophets and Jesus saw future events as we might see two ranges of mountains from a distance. Some of the prophecies were fulfilled in earlier events and some will be fulfilled later, just as one mountain range is closer and one further. But from a distance they seem as if they come together. Jesus' prophecy in this chapter touches on two periods, the fall of Jerusalem (vv. 15-28), and the end of all things (roughly from v. 29 on).

"The elect" mentioned in verses 22, 24 and 31 are God's people. See also Mark 13:20, 22, 27; Romans 11:7; 2 Timothy 2:10; Titus 1:1; 1 Peter 1:1.

Question 11. The lesson of the fig tree is clear enough: just as tender twigs and leaves indicate the nearness of summer, so the presence of "these things" indicate that "it" is near. But what do *these things*, *it* (or *he*) and *this generation* refer to? There are several possibilities. Some interpret *it* as the destruction of Jerusalem and therefore view "these things" as the events preceding its destruction. According to this view, *this generation* refers to the generation alive during the time of Jesus.

Others view *it* (or *he*) as the second coming of Christ and *these things* as the events immediately preceding his return. According to this interpretation, *this generation* refers to the generation alive at the time of the second coming (or possibly to the Jewish race, since the Greek word for *generation* can mean "race"). These verses may be confusing simply because they cannot be restricted solely to one option (the fall of Jerusalem) or the other (the second coming). Perhaps there is both a more immediate fulfilment and a later fulfilment, as in the case of the "abomination that causes desolation" (see note to question 8).

Question 12. *That day* (v. 36) is one of the usual New Testament expressions for the second coming of Jesus.

Study 11. Jesus the Sacrifice. Matthew 26:1-30.

Purpose: To consider the Lord's Supper as a picture of Jesus' death on the cross and our participation in the benefits of his death.

Question 1. Define each of the four sections of the passage and then talk about how Jesus' actions and tone in each.

Question 2. As preparation for the study you may wish to trace how the hostility to Jesus began and grew, and why. See Mark 2:67; 3:2, 22; 7:5; 8:11; 9:14; 10:2; 11:27-28; 12:12-13, 18.

Question 3. Matthew tells us that the perfume was "very expensive" (v. 7). Mark 14:5 says it was worth more than a year's wages (300 denarii).

Jesus' statement about the poor always being with us (v. 11) has been twisted to mean that we should not do anything to try to eliminate poverty. It becomes a rationalization not to help. But clearly Jesus' intention is to indicate that there is always an opportunity and an obligation to help those in poverty.

How is love's extravagance justified? By the beauty of her devotion. By an opportunity that will not always be there. By the ability of the devotee—"she did what she could" (Mk 14:8). And by the spiritual significance of the occasion—in this case Jesus' burial—which has out-of-the-ordinary meaning.

Question 4. See also John 12:4-6. What were Judas' motives? None of the Gospel writers tells us, so the best we can do is reconstruct the events and conjecture about why he betrayed Jesus. We know that the religious leaders were looking for an opportunity to arrest Jesus. They wanted to do so secretly to avoid a riot during the Passover celebration in Jerusalem (Mk 14:12). However, because there were more than 300,000 people in the city (as opposed to its normal population of 50,000) and because Jesus had withdrawn to a village outside Jerusalem (Jn 11:54), the religious leaders had difficulty finding him (Jn 11:56). Therefore, they gave orders "that if anyone found out where Jesus was, he should report it so that they might arrest him" (Jn 11:57).

Of course Judas both knew where Jesus was and when the best opportunity would be to arrest him quietly. Therefore, he went to the chief priests and offered to hand Jesus over for thirty silver coins (about 120 day's wages; Mt 26:15). Why did he do it? Perhaps he was disillusioned with Jesus, who had failed to enter Jerusalem as the conquering Messiah the people expected. Perhaps Judas convinced himself that if he could not share in the messianic power and glory he had hoped for, at least he could salvage some monetary reward. Both Luke and John tell us that "Satan entered Judas" (Lk 22:3; Jn 13:27), who became a pawn in the hands of demonic powers and their attempt to destroy Jesus.

Questions 5-6. See also Mark 14:12; 1 Corinthians 5:7. Throughout the centuries the Passover celebration had symbolically portrayed the death of Christ, "the Lamb of God, who takes away the sin of the world" (Jn 1:29).

If the members of your group are unfamiliar with the Passover, it might be good to have them read the verses in Exodus quickly and silently. However, if someone in the group can briefly summarize the significance of Passover (when it first took place, what took place and so on), that would be better.

Question 8. On the relationship between God's sovereignty and human responsibility, see Acts 2:23. The Scriptures put side by side the statements about God's sovereignty and our responsibility without attempting to reconcile them.

Question 9. Jesus said, "This is my blood of the covenant, which is poured out for many for the forgiveness of sins" (v. 28). The covenant he speaks of is the New Covenant, which replaced the Old Covenant between God and Israel (Ex 24:8). The prophet Jeremiah spoke of a day when God would establish this New Covenant: "'The time is coming,' declares the LORD, 'when I will make a new covenant with the house of Israel and with the house of Judah. It will not be like the covenant I made with their forefathers when I took them by the hand to lead them out of Egypt, because they broke my covenant, though I was a husband to them,' declares the LORD" (Jer 31:31-32). See also Hebrews 8:6-13.

Question 10. Obviously we must interpret the Lord's Supper in light of further New Testament revelation. The event itself only gives us a glimpse and a picture of truths explained much more fully later on. However, it is significant that the symbolism involves not only the bread and wine—pictures of Christ's body and blood—but also the eating and drinking of these elements by his followers. In other words, we must somehow intimately partake of Christ's death in order to participate in its benefits. Eating the bread and drinking the wine, therefore, become symbols of saving faith (see Jn 6:53-63).

Study 12. Jesus the Dying King. John 19:16-42.
Purpose: To be confronted with the fact and significance of Jesus' crucifixion.
Question 2. John's sparing description of the details of the crucifixion could mean that crucifixion was very familiar and needed no elaboration or so horrible that he decided to pass over it. But perhaps it is even more likely that John is seeking to emphasize the spiritual meaning of Jesus' death. If the group struggles with the question, try restating it: "Is this just because crucifixion was a familiar kind of execution, or is John concentrating on something else? Explain."
Question 4. The significance of this inscription was in its irony. Not only was Pilate bitterly embarrassing the Jewish leaders who had put him in an uncomfortable spot, but Jesus truly was to be the King of all the world, as shown by the three languages. The inscription also confirmed the spiritual character of Jesus' kingdom which, as he had told Pilate, was "not of this world" (18:36). "Jesus' claim to royalty was asserted in a new way. . . . He demonstrated his sovereignty by dying, not by fighting" (Merrill Tenney, *John*, p. 266).
Question 5. "The disciple whom he loved" (v. 26) is undoubtedly John, the author of this Gospel. Normally, after the death of the husband and the oldest son, a mother would be cared for by the surviving members of her family. In a cultural sense, therefore, Jesus' action is somewhat unusual. However, his brothers and sisters did not believe in him at this point (Jn 7:5), although they evidently came to faith after the resurrection (Acts 1:14). See also John 1:10-13.
Question 6. "It is finished" (v. 30) was indeed a cry of victory. Jesus was in charge. It was Pilate who was really on trial—and the Jewish leaders, the soldiers and all others in this chapter. Jesus had been fulfilling God's plan. The phrase "It is finished" is the Greek word *tetelestai*, which means, among other things, "paid in full." The price of sin was paid in full. So Jesus actively "bowed his head and gave up his spirit" (v. 30). Jesus had now finished the great work of salvation, had suffered judg-

ment that we might not be judged, and had died that we might live.

The lifting of the sponge on a stalk of the hyssop plant (v. 29) is seen by some commentators as symbolic. Hyssop was used by the Jewish people to sprinkle blood on the doors of their homes the night they were delivered from captivity in Egypt (Ex 12:22). So Jesus here appears as the Lamb of God whose blood is shed for the sins of the world, and thus the true meaning of the Passover is fulfilled.

Question 7. Again, the burial was an important confirmation of the actual death of Jesus. The Koran, for example, states that Jesus did not actually die but swooned and revived. Hugh Schonfield's book *The Passover Plot* also asserts that Jesus did not die but was drugged and consequently survived. But the testimony of the soldiers and of Nicodemus and Joseph, who actually handled Jesus' dead body, confirms the fact of his death. Jewish burial customs did not involve embalming but the simple wrapping of a dead body in linen cloths, covered with heavy layers of spices (v. 40).

Question 8. Merrill Tenney suggests that each group in this chapter represented the belief or unbelief of some class of person. The Jewish leaders showed the unbelief of religion which had turned into pride and prejudice. Pilate showed the unbelief of political expediency. The solders rolling dice were a picture of callousness and indifference. On the other hand, the women by the cross showed belief through their loyalty and love. And Nicodemus and Joseph show how true faith will draw us into the open, from secret discipleship to openly following Jesus.

Question 10. The division of the garments (vv. 23-24) was not exceptionally brutal. It was a common practice. But this seemly insignificant event shows that Jesus' death was a fulfillment of Old Testament prophecy. Jesus was not a helpless victim. He was actively fulfilling the plan and purpose of God in becoming the Savior of the world by his death.

Question 11. The executioners broke the legs of victims (vv. 32-33) to hasten their death. Unable to support themselves on broken legs, the asphyxiation which crucifixion involved would become more intense. No doubt John mentions this episode because it is important evidence that Jesus actually died. These soldiers were expert executioners. They knew the difference between death and coma. Likewise, the piercing of Jesus' side and the flow of blood and water (serum) is proof that death had happened. Only blood would flow from a living body. The water and blood could also have been a result of piercing the pericardium (the sac that surrounds the heart) and the heart itself.

Study 13. Jesus the Risen Lord. John 20.

Purpose: To examine the evidence for the resurrection of Jesus.

Question 2. The "other disciple" is thought to be John, the author of this Gospel.

Stone tombs were closed by circular stones set in slanting grooves in which the stone would roll into place. It would take the strength of several men to open it. The women did not expect it to be rolled away and could not have done it by themselves. It must have been moved by some strong force and for a purpose.

The empty tomb is an important evidence for the resurrection. It was only a short distance from where the first Christians preached that Jesus was risen, and anyone could easily have gone to check out whether or not the tomb was in fact empty.

It is hard to believe that the disciples stole the body, for Peter and the other disciple would hardly have come running to see a tomb they knew was empty. Nor would they likely have died later for preaching something they knew was not true. And if enemies stole the body, why did they not try to produce the evidence when they were later trying to discredit the Christians?

The grave cloths (vv. 6-7) are also significant, especially since John describes them as lying there essentially undisturbed. The cloths were intact and collapsed by the weight of the spices, but the body was gone. The napkin which had been around Jesus' head was folded up and lying by itself where his head would have been. How could anyone have stolen the body and left the grave cloths like that?

Question 3. None of these witnesses of the resurrection were expecting to see Jesus. When Mary saw him, she thought he was the gardener (v. 15). Luke tells us that when the disciples in the Upper Room saw Jesus, they were "startled and frightened, thinking they saw a ghost" (Lk 24:37). And Thomas clearly did not expect to have any proof that Jesus actually was risen (v. 25). So the personal appearances of Jesus can hardly be explained on the basis of hallucination, when the disciples neither expected nor believed he would rise.

Mary's not recognizing Jesus (v. 14) may indicate that his appearance was, at least to some extent, changed. However, we should also keep in mind that it was early in the morning, Mary was crying, and evidently she didn't fully turn toward Jesus until he said "Mary" (v. 16).

Jesus' order to Mary "Do not hold on to me" (v. 17) seems to indicate that he wants his disciples to depend less on his physical presence and more on their new spiritual relationship.

Question 4. Verse 23 should literally be translated as: "Those whose sins you forgive have already been forgiven; those whose sins you do not forgive have not been forgiven." God's forgiveness was not and is not conditional upon our forgiveness. Rather the apostles (and we today) have the authority to declare that those who have believed in Jesus have been forgiven and those who have not believed in Jesus have not been forgiven.

Question 6. Here we have a marvelous example both of Jesus' authority and his compassion. He knew what Thomas had said. He was able to pass through locked doors. Yet he did not so much rebuke Thomas as show compassion and give him evidence on which to believe.

Question 7. For a Jew to call another man "Lord and God" (v. 28) meant that he had come to worship him as true deity.

Question 8. If you have time, a good follow-up question to discuss would be: "Is faith belief without evidence? belief based on evidence? commitment that goes beyond evidence? Explain."

Leighton Ford heads Leighton Ford Ministries, which seeks to help young leaders worldwide to lead more like Jesus and more to Jesus. For many years he communicated Christ worldwide through speaking, writing and the media. He describes his current mission to be "an artist of the soul and a friend on the journey."